"Who will help me pick the apples?"

3

4   "Who will help me wash the apples?"

"Who will help me peel the apples?"

"Who will help me cut the apples?"

"Not me!" said the cow.

"Not me!" said the duck.
"Not me!" said the rabbit.

"Who will help me cook the apples?"

13

15